TO SYLVIA BOORSTEIN, AT SPIRIT ROCK,
WHO TAUGHT ME TO SING MY LOVING-KINDNESS MEDITATION.

Bala Kids
An imprint of Shambhala Publications, Inc.
2129 13th Street
Boulder, Colorado 80302
www.shambhala.com

Text © 2023 by Susan B. Katz
Illustrations © 2023 by Jennie Poh

Cover art by Jennie Poh
Design by Kara Plikaitis

9 8 7 6 5 4 3 2 1

First Edition
Printed in Malaysia

Shambhala Publications makes every effort to print on acid-free, recycled paper.
Bala Kids is distributed worldwide by Penguin Random House, Inc., and its subsidiaries.

Library of Congress Cataloging-in-Publication Data
Names: Katz, Susan B., 1971– author. | Poh, Jennie, translator.
Title: Share your love / Susan B. Katz; illustrated by Jennie Poh.
Description: First edition. | Boulder, Colorado : Bala Kids, an imprint of Shambhala Publications, Inc.,
[2023] | Includes author's note.
Identifiers: LCCN 2021055965 | ISBN 9781645471110 (hardcover)
Subjects: CYAC: Stories in rhyme. | Meditation—Fiction. | Mindfulness (Psychology)—Fiction. | Love—
Fiction. | LCGFT: Picture books. | Stories in rhyme.
Classification: LCC PZ8.3.K1284 Sh 2023 | DDC [E]—dc23
LC record available at https://lccn.loc.gov/2021055965

SHARE
YOUR
LOVE

Susan B. Katz

Illustrated by Jennie Poh

bala kids

You have so much love
in your one little heart.
Send it out to the world.
It's easy—let's start.

You can send a kind thought
to yourself and to others,
like your parents, teachers,
sisters, or brothers.

No coins in a fountain
or stars in the sky.
First wish yourself kindness.
Let's give it a try.

You are worthy of love.
So just put on a smile.
To make yourself happy,
sing this once in a while:

"May I be protected and safe.
May I feel happy and pleased.
May my body be healthy,
and may I live with ease."

Take a breath in and out,
and again when it ends.
Who else can you wish well?
Your family or friends?

Think of your mom,
dad, grandma, or pet.
Pick one special being,
anyone that you've met.

"May you be protected and safe.
May you feel happy and pleased.
May your body be healthy,
and may you live with ease."

Who might be next
in this magical task?
You don't need to tell me.
I won't ever ask.

"May you be protected and safe.
May you feel happy and pleased.
May your body be healthy,
and may you live with ease."

Sing for your sister,
brother, uncle, or cousin.
It might take a while
if you have a dozen.

What about your
neighbor?
Or art teacher at school?
Sharing love is like magic.
It's your invisible tool!

"May you be protected and safe.
May you feel happy and pleased.
May your body be healthy,
and may you live with ease."

Now comes the hard part,
but it's like giving a gift!
Sing to someone you don't like
so your angry thoughts shift.

"May you be protected and safe.
May you feel happy and pleased.
May your body be healthy,
and may you live with ease."

Don't you feel better?
Sharing love, wishing well?
It's lighter than worry
and makes your heart swell.

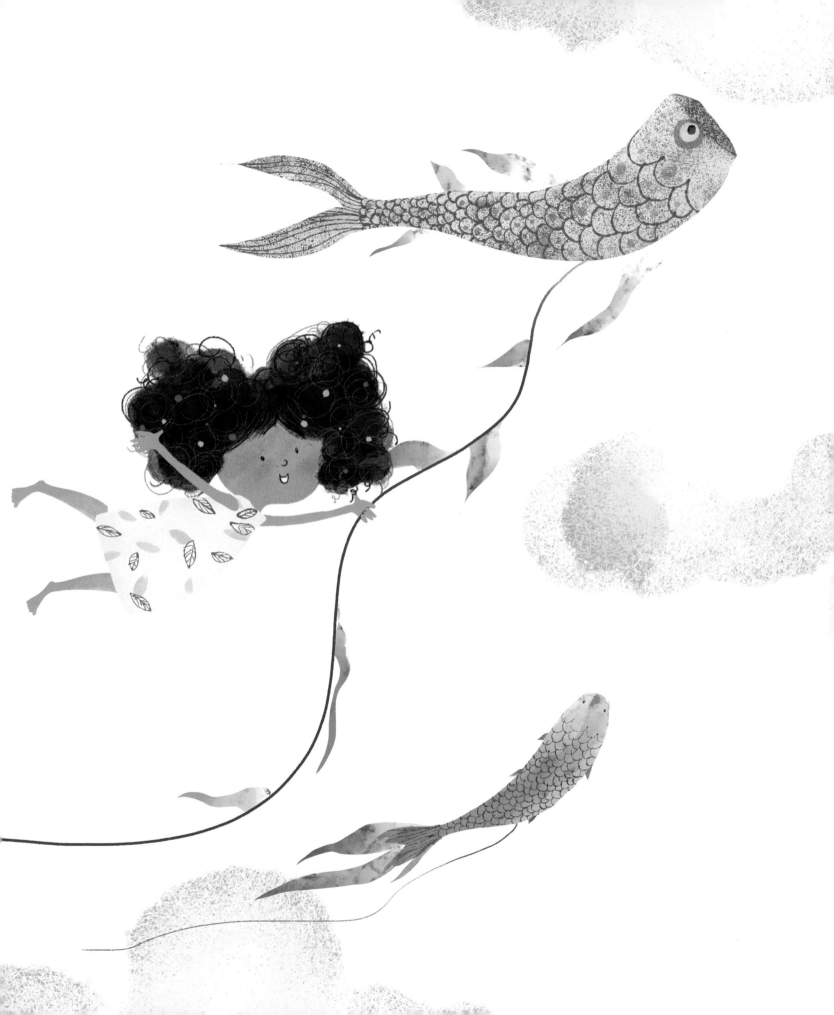

Now come back to yourself,
like a circle complete.
Picture a white light around you
from your head to your feet.

"May I be protected and safe.
May I feel happy and pleased.
May my body be healthy,
and may I live with ease."

You are worthy of love.
So are all people world round.

Sing for all living creatures,
above and below ground.

Send out your well-wishes.
No need to use words.
Your mind can help heal
snails, crickets, and birds!

From the treetops in forests
to deep in the sea,

may all living beings
be happy and free!

Keep sharing your love
from morning till night.

See the change you can make
with a love that shines bright.

Author's Note

How can we share our love without even being in the same room to hug someone? Whether you are feeling worried or sad, grateful or mad, you can silently send good wishes out to your friends and family through your thoughts. You start by calming your mind and healing your heart. If you are confused or lonely, sing (to the tune of "Happy Birthday to You"):

May I be protected and safe.
May I feel happy and pleased.
May my body be healthy,
and may I live with ease.

You can help heal the world by hoping that all beings are safe, happy, healthy, and calm.

Sharing my love with loving-kindness (Metta) meditation has helped me through very tough times. I even stretch my mind, and heart, to share love with difficult people in my life. I like to sing my well-wishes, because it makes it more pleasant to repeat a song in my head. But you can just say it, too. The important thing is that we can send out positive thoughts to heal beings all over the world just by sitting still and sharing our love. Your mind is magical, and your heart can heal!

—SBK